Original title:
I Found Myself

Copyright © 2024 Swan Charm
All rights reserved.

Author: Paula Raudsepp
ISBN HARDBACK: 978-9916-79-024-3
ISBN PAPERBACK: 978-9916-79-025-0
ISBN EBOOK: 978-9916-79-026-7

A Rebirth of the Soul's Flame

In shadows deep, a whisper's song,
A flicker glows where it belongs.
Through weary nights, the heart awakes,
To grasp the light that softly breaks.

From ashes cold, the embers rise,
Beneath the weight of silent skies.
Each spark a tale of love and grace,
A dance of hope, a warm embrace.

The winds of change begin to stir,
With every breath, the spirits purr.
A symphony of silent dreams,
As radiant as the morning beams.

In gardens lush, the colors bloom,
As life dispels the sense of gloom.
With every heartbeat, courage flows,
A stirring strength that ever grows.

A journey bright, a path untold,
Where time bestows its gifts of gold.
With open hearts, we rise anew,
As flames entwine in vivid hue.

The Canvas of Being

Brush strokes form the dawn,
Colors blend and sway,
Each hue a silent song,
Life in bright array.

From shadows come the light,
Shaping whispers, bold,
In the quiet night,
Stories yet untold.

Textures weave the fate,
Captured in the glance,
Moments here await,
To dance in chance's dance.

In every shade, a dream,
In every line, a voice,
The canvas holds the theme,
Of choice and joy's rejoice.

So let the colors speak,
Let the heart take flight,
For in this art we seek,
The essence of our light.

Fragments of a Whole

Pieces scattered wide,
Lost in time's embrace,
Yet in fragments hide,
The truth of our space.

Mirror shards reflect,
Glimpses of the past,
In their sharp defect,
Memories hold fast.

Each fragment has a edge,
A story to be told,
Upon life's great ledge,
We build, brave and bold.

Connecting every part,
With threads made of care,
We find a shared heart,
In love's gentle glare.

Embracing all the pain,
We rise from the fall,
In the whole remains,
The beauty of it all.

In Search of Lost Light

Wander through the mist,
Chasing shadows long,
Yearning for a tryst,
With a forgotten song.

Stars flicker and fade,
Lost in the night's sigh,
In the truth we wade,
Reaching for the sky.

Memory's soft glow,
Guides the weary hand,
Through the silent woe,
And the endless sand.

Hope will guide the way,
Through the darkest hour,
Bringing dawn's first ray,
With a gentle power.

In the depths we find,
Light that will not die,
Illuminating mind,
As the spirits fly.

The Awakening Dream

In twilight's embrace,
Dreams begin to bloom,
Awakening the space,
Where shadows find room.

Whispers drift in air,
Soft and full of light,
Calling hearts to dare,
To step out of night.

In this gentle morn,
Hope takes its first breath,
From the dreamer's thorn,
To a life from death.

Colors spill and weave,
Patterns in the sky,
With each thread we breathe,
Through the clouds we fly.

This dream is a gift,
To those who believe,
In the heart's swift lift,
And the joys we weave.

A Quest for Wholeness

In valleys deep, where shadows play,
I wander forth, both night and day.
With every step, I seek the light,
And piece together my inner fight.

The mountains call, their peaks so high,
I yearn to soar, to touch the sky.
Yet in the still, the truth unfolds,
Wholeness resides in the heart it holds.

Through rivers wide and forests dense,
I search for love, seek recompense.
The whispers of the wind remind,
That peace is found when hearts align.

With open arms, embracing grace,
I meet the world, I find my place.
Each fragment lost, now gathered near,
In this great quest, I hold no fear.

For in the journey, I discover,
The path leads home, a sacred cover.
In every struggle, in every loss,
I rise anew, no matter the cost.

The Colors of Me

In the morning sun, I feel alive,
A palette bright where dreams contrive.
With every hue, my spirit sings,
The colors blend, what joy it brings.

Deep azure blue, my calm and peace,
Emerald green, where worries cease.
Crimson red, of passion's fire,
Golden yellow, my heart's desire.

Every shade a story told,
In vibrant strokes, I break the mold.
Lavender whispers, soft and sweet,
While indigo dances in the heat.

A canvas vast, my life unfolds,
In every shade, my soul beholds.
Through storms and sun, I paint my way,
Embracing colors day by day.

With every brush, the strokes resound,
An artist's heart, where love is found.
The colors of me, forever bright,
In every moment, pure delight.

Serendipity's Child

Beneath the stars, where fortune lies,
I chase the dreams that spark the skies.
The paths I tread, so unplanned,
With open heart, I take a stand.

In chance encounters, magic brews,
A gentle hint, a chance to choose.
With every twist, the world aligns,
In serendipity, my spirit shines.

Through unexpected turns and bends,
I find the joy that freely lends.
The laughter shared, the smiles exchanged,
In these moments, life is changed.

Let faith be my guiding light,
As I embrace both day and night.
For in the simple, grand I see,
A tapestry of destiny.

Serendipity, my faithful guide,
With every step, I bloom with pride.
In life's sweet dance, I trust and play,
For joy awaits along the way.

The Light Beyond the Veil

In shadows deep, where fears abide,
I search for truth, no need to hide.
With courage firm, I lift the veil,
To find the light that will prevail.

The whispers soft, they call my name,
In hidden realms, there is no shame.
A luminescence, warm and bright,
Awakens hope, dispels the night.

The journey starts with breath so slow,
Each step I take, more love I sow.
For in the quiet, I hear the call,
The light within can conquer all.

With every heartbeat, I grow wise,
Unraveling all that underlies.
In stillness found, I start to see,
The beauty shines, it's right inside me.

Beyond the veil, the world expands,
With open heart, I understand.
The light is love, the truth revealed,
In every soul, it is concealed.

Threads of Identity

In shadows deep, we weave our tale,
With whispers soft, our truths unveil.
Each thread a story, rich and bright,
A tapestry formed in the dead of night.

Yet in the light, we find our form,
A dance of colors where hearts are warm.
Connected souls through joy and strife,
Threads of identity, woven life.

In every stitch, a memory lies,
In laughter's echo, in silent cries.
Together we build, a grand design,
Threads of identity, uniquely divine.

As the fabric grows, so does our song,
Each note a piece where we belong.
In unity, stronger we stand,
Threads of identity, hand in hand.

Awakening the Silent Song

In sleeping hearts, a melody waits,
An echo true that love creates.
Beneath the surface, silence gleams,
Awakening softly, like whispered dreams.

With every breath, the notes align,
A symphony born from the divine.
In shadows cast, the voices rise,
Awakening the silent song, no disguise.

As dawn breaks through the night's embrace,
The silent song finds its rightful place.
In harmony's sway, we bloom and grow,
Awakening the silent song, set to flow.

With courage drawn from depths unknown,
We sing the truths we've always grown.
In vibrant tones, our spirits soar,
Awakening the silent song once more.

A Tapestry of Lost Dreams

In quiet corners of forgotten minds,
Lie threads of passion, true love that binds.
A tapestry woven with hopes once bright,
Now faded shadows, lost in the night.

Each dream a story, told in dust,
With vibrant colors turned to rust.
Yet in the stillness, whispers remain,
A tapestry of lost dreams, not in vain.

We gather remnants, piecing the past,
Reviving echoes, shadows they cast.
Through longing hearts and silent screams,
A tapestry of lost dreams, stitched with seams.

With every thread, we learn and see,
Embracing losses that set us free.
In the beauty of scars, truths redeem,
A tapestry of lost dreams, once deemed.

Embracing the Uncharted

In the heart of unknown, adventure calls,
Beyond the borders where shadows fall.
With courage rising, we take that leap,
Embracing the uncharted, a dream to keep.

Through winding paths and forests wide,
In every heartbeat, we choose to ride.
With open minds and eager hearts,
Embracing the uncharted, art that starts.

The siren sings of realms untold,
Of secrets waiting, treasures of gold.
In the depths of doubt, our spirits sing,
Embracing the uncharted, it's everything.

With every step, we break the mold,
The light of courage makes us bold.
Together as one, we chart the skies,
Embracing the uncharted, where freedom lies.

The Breath of New Beginnings

In the dawn's soft light, dreams arise,
With each gentle breeze, the spirit flies.
A canvas fresh, untouched by time,
Hope paints its hues, a life to climb.

Each heartbeat stirs the yearning soul,
In every moment, we find our goal.
Let go of shadows, embrace the day,
For new beginnings, guide our way.

The past is but a whisper's echo,
A flicker of light in the undertow.
Step forward boldly, chase the sun,
In the dance of life, we are all one.

With every breath, a chance to grow,
In the garden of dreams, new seeds we sow.
The horizon calls with colors bright,
In this sacred space, we ignite.

So cherish the dawn, with open hands,
In the heart of change, true power stands.
Each new beginning, a sacred trust,
In the breath of life, we rise from dust.

In the Silence Between Heartbeats

A hush lingers softly in the night,
Where thoughts entwine, a spark of light.
In the stillness, whispers take flight,
The universe sings, hidden from sight.

Moments drift like clouds in the sky,
In the pause between breaths, we sigh.
Each heartbeat whispers secrets untold,
In the silence, our spirits unfold.

Lost in contemplation, time seems to pause,
Finding the rhythm in nature's laws.
In the quiet, we learn to feel,
The heartbeat of life, vibrant and real.

Resting in stillness, the world fades away,
In the calm embrace, night turns to day.
Awakening dreams in the softest sigh,
In the silence, we learn to fly.

Listen closely to the echoes around,
In each silence, a promise is found.
A symphony waits in the softest breath,
In the quietude, we conquer death.

Unmasking the Real Me

Behind the facade, a truth resides,
Layers of stories that love divides.
With courage as my steadfast guide,
I shed the masks that I once hide.

Each peel reveals a tender scar,
A glimpse of light, a shining star.
What once felt shame, now blooms with grace,
In vulnerability, I find my place.

The journey of self, both fierce and kind,
In brokenness, I no longer blind.
Authenticity sings, a beautiful song,
In the heart of truth, I finally belong.

With every breath, I embrace the fight,
To walk in my truth, to own my light.
In the quiet courage of being free,
I unmask the essence of the real me.

Together we rise, in the warmth of love,
Guided by stars from the heavens above.
In the dance of acceptance, I find my peace,
Unmasking the self, a sweet release.

The Symphony of Inner Whispers

Soft murmurs flow like a gentle stream,
Carving paths through the fabric of dream.
An orchestra of thoughts, sweet and pure,
In the stillness, the heart finds its cure.

Each note resonates, a tale it weaves,
In the echoes of silence, the spirit believes.
With harmonies wrapped in twilight's glow,
The symphony of whispers begins to grow.

Hidden insights rise to the surface,
In the melody of life, we find purpose.
In every pause, a chance to hear,
The subtle whispers that draw us near.

Each chord a memory, each rhythm a spark,
Illuminating the soft and the dark.
With every whisper, our souls align,
In the symphony of life, we truly shine.

So listen closely to the song within,
In the chamber of heart, where it begins.
For in those whispers, we find our way,
The symphony of whispers guides the day.

Beyond the Surface Glimmer

Beneath the waves of silent dreams,
A world awaits, not as it seems.
Ripples dance in morning light,
A whisper calls, ignites the night.

Emerald depths hold secrets tight,
Fish that weave through shadows bright.
Each flicker tells a tale untold,
Of treasures waiting, brave and bold.

Around the coral, colors play,
In gentle currents, hearts sway.
Magic twirls in ocean's song,
Inviting all to come along.

The horizon meets the azure skies,
Where dreams ascend and hope can rise.
In every glance, a spark ignites,
Beyond the surface, pure delights.

So dive within and take a chance,
In hidden realms where spirits dance.
For in the depths, life's riches gleam,
And every wish becomes a dream.

A Ballet of Becoming

In shadows cast by twilight's glow,
A tender grace begins to flow.
Dancers twirl through time's embrace,
Each movement finds its rightful place.

The stage adorned with hopes and fears,
Reveals the story through the years.
With every step, the heart takes flight,
A ballet born of day and night.

The rhythm pulses, life's sweet song,
As shadows shift and spirits throng.
Weaving dreams in silken threads,
Painting paths where courage treads.

A swirling dress, a fleeting glance,
Each spin a chance, a whispered chance.
In this dance, we learn to see,
The beauty of what's meant to be.

So let us move with hearts ablaze,
In every moment, set the stage.
For life's a dance, a grand display,
A ballet of becoming, come what may.

When the Fabric of Self Unravels

Threads of identity come apart,
In the quiet corners of the heart.
Each fraying edge reveals a new,
A glimpse of self once thought to be true.

In the stillness, echoes of pain,
Whisper stories, like falling rain.
Memories linger, color the air,
Pieces scattered everywhere.

Time weaves gently, redefines,
What once was lost in shifting signs.
Through the chaos, clarity forms,
In life's storms, new beauty warms.

Unraveling threads can lead to light,
Through shadowed paths, a hopeful sight.
Every strand, a lesson learned,
In the fires of life, resilience burned.

So stitch together, piece by piece,
Embrace the journey, find your peace.
For within unravelling lies the grace,
Of becoming whole, a sacred space.

Mapping the Heart's Geography

Across the canvas of the soul,
Each heartbeat shapes the hidden whole.
In valleys deep, where feelings flow,
A map unfolds, a tale to know.

Adventure paths through joy and pain,
Winding roads like gentle rain.
In every sunrise, love ignites,
Charting stars on endless nights.

Mountains rise with dreams in bloom,
While rivers sing to the heart's tune.
Footprints mark where we have been,
In every pause, new stories spin.

The compass turns, the heart finds way,
Navigating night and day.
With every leap, the spirit soars,
Mapping the heart, forever explores.

So gather round and draw your lines,
In sacred spaces, where love shines.
For in this journey, we shall see,
The heart's geography will set us free.

Embracing the Shadows of Yesterday

In the quiet dusk, memories call,
Whispers of laughter, shadows of fall.
Hiding in corners, they dance and sway,
Guiding my heart, they show me the way.

Time's gentle hands weave stories of gold,
Secrets of love in the silence unfold.
Lessons are carved in the stone of the past,
Embrace every moment, for none can outlast.

Beneath the darkness, light starts to creep,
Awakening dreams that once lay asleep.
Forgiveness and hope rise from the deep,
In shadows of yesterday, my soul learns to leap.

The pain and the joy, they coexist here,
Drawing me closer, dispelling my fear.
I honor each memory, letting them flow,
Embracing the shadows, together we grow.

Treading on Unfamiliar Ground

With each step forward, the earth feels strange,
Paths untraveled, horizons to change.
Braving the unknown, I find my own beat,
A dance in the wild, where hope and fear meet.

Textures of silence, and colors anew,
Footprints of courage in morning's dew.
Every falter teaches, as I learn to stand,
In the vastness around, with only my hand.

Winds whisper secrets, guiding me through,
Echoes of wisdom in every hue.
Nature's embrace, both fierce and kind,
Filling my spirit with beauty entwined.

Clarity blossoms amid the unknown,
In the depths of confusion, I've brightly grown.
Treading on paths that challenge my soul,
With each step onward, I feel more whole.

The Invisible Tides of Transformation

Waves of intention crash upon shore,
Carving my essence, I am evermore.
Silent but potent, the currents they sweep,
Waking my spirit from slumber so deep.

In the depths of change, I dance and I sway,
Shifting like sand, yet here I will stay.
Invisible forces, like breath on the skin,
Pulling and pushing, the journey begins.

Ripples of growth emanate within,
Each moment a seed, all change can begin.
Embracing the waves as they rise and they fall,
Listening closely, I hear the call.

Transformation's tide, a constant refrain,
Through storms and through sunshine, lessons remain.
I flow with acceptance, an ocean so wide,
In the heart of the tides, my truth will abide.

An Unseen Journey to Clarity

In the fog of the mind, a whisper appears,
Guiding my steps through the maze of my fears.
Invisible pathways unfold in the mist,
A promise of clarity, I cannot resist.

The heart's quiet compass points ever true,
Drawing me forward in shades of deep blue.
With patience I tread, on this road made of dreams,
Seeking the light where illusion redeems.

Every stumble teaches, every pause refines,
Moments of doubt become treasures that shine.
Each breath a reminder, I'm not alone,
In the depths of uncertainty, strength has been grown.

With each step awakened, I gather my grace,
Finding the courage to embrace each place.
An unseen journey, yet so vividly clear,
Filling my heart with both wonder and cheer.

Breaking the Surface

Beneath the waves so vast and deep,
Lies a world where silence keeps.
Ripples whisper, secrets flow,
Hints of wonders we do not know.

In the depths, shadows dance and play,
Guiding lost souls on their way.
Sunbeams filter through the blue,
Awakening dreams that feel so true.

The surface trembles, a gentle sigh,
Echoes of life as time drifts by.
Breath of the ocean, calm and wide,
Invites the heart to drift inside.

As tides change, the hidden emerge,
From the depths, life's vibrant surge.
Surface broken, new paths wind,
In the quiet, clarity we find.

Let go the fears that bind the soul,
Embrace the tides that make us whole.
In every splash, a story told,
Of journeys ventured, brave and bold.

The Unseen Tapestry

Threads of fate, woven in time,
Colors blend, a rhythm, a rhyme.
Patterns form where eyes can't see,
Life's design, a mystery.

In the fabric, shadows play,
Moments lost, yet here they stay.
Unraveled paths, a story spun,
Each a thread, together run.

Hands that weave in joy and strife,
Stitching together the fabric of life.
In every knot, a tale unfolds,
Of warmth and strength, of hearts so bold.

The unseen binds us, thread by thread,
In the loom of life, love is spread.
Though unseen, the bond is true,
A tapestry made just for you.

As we hold our stories tight,
Together we weave day and night.
In the tapestry, we find our place,
A colorful world, a warm embrace.

Mosaic of the Mind

Fragments scattered, bright and bold,
A vivid tale, a story told.
Thoughts collide, colors mix,
Creating dreams, a canvas fixed.

In every piece, a spark ignites,
Fleeting thoughts, like fireflies.
Together forming, a larger view,
A patchwork made from me and you.

Whispers echo, voices blend,
In this mosaic, we transcend.
Shattered pieces, beauty defined,
In every corner, treasure mined.

Embrace the chaos, find the grace,
In this journey, we find our space.
Mosaic smiles, we wear with pride,
In the mind's gallery, dreams reside.

As we collect each shining part,
We build a world, we find a heart.
A mosaic gleams in life's embrace,
Each piece a part of time and space.

Gleaning the Unspoken

Silent words hang in the air,
Emotions deep, we feel and share.
Unseen whispers guide the way,
In the stillness, truth will sway.

Glimmers of thought, wrapped in dreams,
Beyond the surface, nothing's as it seems.
Listening close, the heart can learn,
In the quiet, bridges burn.

What is left unsaid remains,
A haunting melody, that still gains.
In every pause, a chance to grow,
Gleaning wisdom in the flow.

Eyes that speak, a knowing glance,
Beneath the silence, souls advance.
In unspoken words, we find our part,
A language crafted from the heart.

So linger here, in this soft space,
Glean the beauty, find your grace.
In every breath, the depth unfolds,
In unspoken dreams, the truth beholds.

Whispers of the Heart

In shadows where secrets lie,
The heart speaks soft, a gentle sigh.
Echoes of dreams, both bright and dim,
In quiet moments, hopes swim.

Through tangled paths where feelings roam,
Each whisper calls like a distant home.
Tender whispers that time can't erase,
In the silence, we find our place.

Fleeting glances in a crowded room,
A language spoken in quiet bloom.
Promises wrapped in the evening's glow,
In the heart's chamber, love will grow.

With every beat, a story unfolds,
A tapestry of warmth to hold.
Threads of passion, threads of care,
In whispers, our truths we share.

As night descends, the stars awake,
Their silent song, the heart will take.
In the stillness, dreams take flight,
Whispers of the heart, pure delight.

Embracing the Unknown

In the stillness of the night,
We gather courage, hearts alight.
The path ahead, a mystery wound,
In shadows deep, new dreams are found.

Each step we take, a chance embraced,
In every fear, a truth we traced.
With open arms, we greet the dawn,
For in the unknown, we are reborn.

The winds may change, the skies may pour,
Yet in our hearts, we long for more.
Adventures call, a siren's song,
In leaps of faith, we grow strong.

Beneath the stars, our dreams take flight,
In the chaos, we find our light.
With every heartbeat, we redefine,
Embracing each turn, our spirits shine.

In the journey's breath, we find our peace,
With every step, our doubts decrease.
Through the shadows, our souls will roam,
In the unknown, we find our home.

Unraveled Threads

Once woven tight, now frayed and bare,
Life's tapestry shows tales of despair.
Threads of laughter, threads of tears,
In each unravel, a lifetime nears.

Lost in moments, forgotten dreams,
In faded colors, silent screams.
Yet through the mess, a beauty thrives,
In tangled paths, the spirit survives.

Every knot tells a story true,
Of battles fought, of skies so blue.
With tender hands, we weave anew,
In the chaos, we learn what's due.

From broken strands, new patterns form,
In the wildness, our hearts keep warm.
With every twist, a chance to mend,
In unraveled threads, we find our blend.

And as we stitch our lives along,
The fabric grows, both weak and strong.
Embracing flaws, we find our stride,
In the threads, our truths abide.

Reflections in Still Water

Beneath the surface, calm and clear,
A world awaits, both far and near.
Mirrored skies and whispered trees,
In still water, the heart finds ease.

Each ripple tells a story deep,
Of fleeting moments, memories to keep.
In quiet depths, our spirits dive,
In reflections, we learn to thrive.

The twilight dances on the lake,
In gentle waves, our worries break.
As shadows play and sunbeams glide,
In still water, our dreams reside.

With every glance into the blue,
We see the essence of me and you.
In tranquil pauses, we unearth grace,
Reflections in still water, our embrace.

So let our fears be washed away,
In liquid glass, we choose to stay.
For in these depths, we find our truth,
In still water, forever youth.

Through the Mist, I Walked

Through the misty veil, I tread,
Whispers linger, softly spread.
Shadows dance in twilight's glow,
Steps uncertain, where to go.

Fingers trace the cool, damp air,
Echoes beckon, a silent prayer.
Nature's breath, a tender sigh,
Guiding me beneath the sky.

With each footfall, I feel the ground,
In this realm of dreams unbound.
Crimson hues in fading light,
Leading me through the night.

Moments lost in the shrouded haze,
Fleeting thoughts in the twilight glaze.
Mysteries of the heart unfold,
Stories whispered, yet untold.

And as the dawn begins to break,
Hope ignites with each step I take.
Through the mist, a path appears,
A journey formed through doubts and fears.

Reclaiming My Voice in the Silence

In the quiet corners of my mind,
A voice long lost, I hope to find.
Echoes ring where shadows fall,
Whispers stretching, pleading call.

Tremors rise from depths inside,
Fears dissolve like morning tide.
Words once choked, now break apart,
From the silence, I will start.

Courage blooms within my chest,
A fervent flame, a vibrant quest.
Each syllable, both brave and bold,
Reclaim the stories yet untold.

In gentle roars, I'll cast away,
The chains of silence, here to stay.
Vibrations dance upon my lips,
In this melody, my spirit lifts.

I rise anew with every sound,
In the echoes, strength is found.
Reclaiming what was once my choice,
I'll sing again, I'll find my voice.

The Phoenix from Ashes

From the ashes, a spark ignites,
In the darkness, dreams take flight.
Wings unfurl, the fire glows,
Rising high where the wild wind blows.

Once laid low, now standing tall,
Embers whisper, breaking the fall.
The heart beats with a newfound grace,
In the embrace of a warm embrace.

In the storm, I learned to soar,
In the pain, I found the core.
With each flame, I shed the past,
Transformed and free, the die is cast.

Beauty blooms from charred remains,
In every loss, a truth remains.
Life anew, fierce and bright,
A phoenix born from endless night.

As the skies stretch wide and vast,
I'll take my flight, break free at last.
A vibrant dance in the sun's glow,
From the ashes, I rise and grow.

In the Labyrinth of the Mind

Winding paths and twists unfurl,
In my thoughts, a secret whirl.
Labyrinthine, shadows creep,
Where the silence dares not sleep.

Voices echo, faint and far,
Lost and seeking, who they are.
Each turn a question, every sigh,
In tangled webs, my dreams do lie.

Paths obscure by doubt and fear,
Yet in the maze, a truth draws near.
Illuminating flickers bright,
Moments glimpsed in fleeting light.

Step by step, I journey deep,
Finding treasures hidden in sleep.
Through barren halls, I weave and wind,
Discovering the strength I find.

In this maze, I cease to roam,
Within my heart, I carve a home.
In the labyrinth, hope will bind,
The threads of peace in my own mind.

A Journey Beyond the Veil

In whispers soft, the night calls out,
Where dreams and echoes swirl about.
Footsteps tread on paths unknown,
A quest for truth, the seeds are sown.

Through misty realms, we dare to roam,
With hearts as guides, we'll find our home.
The stars above, they light the way,
To realms where shadows blend and sway.

Among the veils of time and space,
We seek the warmth of love's embrace.
Each breath, a step towards the light,
A journey born from darkest night.

In silence deep, the answers lie,
We reach for stars in the vast sky.
With every hope, we dare to rise,
Beyond the veil, a new sunrise.

So journey forth with open hearts,
Embrace the magic, play your parts.
For life's a dance, a wondrous weave,
In every beat, we shall believe.

Beneath Layers of Dust

In corners dark, where shadows creep,
Memories linger, secrets keep.
Beneath the dust, the stories dwell,
Of laughter lost and tears that fell.

The faded notes of songs once sung,
Echo in halls where hope was flung.
Each trinket tells a tale untold,
Of dreams deferred and hearts turned cold.

With gentle hands, we brush away,
The remnants of a brighter day.
Reclaim the treasures, bold and true,
For in the past, we find our view.

The layers thick, yet light can break,
Reviving dreams that time would shake.
The dust may settle, but hearts will rise,
To reclaim joy beneath the skies.

So lift the veil of dust and grime,
And breathe in deep the rich sublime.
For in the ruins, beauty's found,
A tapestry of love unbound.

Wandering Through My Own Shadows

In twilight's glow, I roam alone,
With shadows cast, I've overgrown.
Each whisper soft, a haunting sound,
In every corner, fears abound.

Yet through the dark, a flicker gleams,
A promise held in distant dreams.
I dance with phantoms, face my fears,
And trace the path of lingering tears.

Awakening truths in silence deep,
I find the strength to wake from sleep.
For shadows speak of lessons learned,
In darkest moments, courage burned.

With open heart, I navigate,
The winding road of love and fate.
Through every twist, I find my way,
To brighter dawns, to lighter days.

So wander on through night's embrace,
For shadows hold a sacred space.
In every step, a light I find,
A journey true, a peace of mind.

The Road Back to My Heart

Upon the path where echoes tread,
I feel the weight of what I've shed.
Each step I take, a chance to heal,
And find the truth in how I feel.

Through winding trails and fields of dreams,
The beauty flows in gentle streams.
With every mile, the burdens lift,
As hope reveals a precious gift.

I gather strength from all I've lost,
Embracing love despite the cost.
The road ahead is bright and wide,
With open arms, I'll walk with pride.

With every heartbeat, feel the spark,
And chase the light that once was dark.
For in the journey, I will find,
A map of love, a heart enshrined.

So take my hand, we'll walk as one,
In this sweet dance, our battles won.
The road back leads to light and grace,
To home within, to love's embrace.

The Geography of Emotions

In valleys deep where shadows play,
Whispers of joy find their way.
Mountains rise, heavy with care,
While rivers of sorrow flow everywhere.

The sky blushes with shades of despair,
Clouds gather thick, they linger there.
Yet sunbeams pierce through the gray,
Illuminating hearts turned to clay.

Desert winds carry dreams long lost,
Each grain of sand counts the cost.
Oceans roar, tides pull and sway,
As emotions mix in a wild ballet.

On streets of hope, footsteps align,
Each heartbeat a rhythm, a sign.
From depths of pain, blooms arise,
Painting the landscape with vibrant skies.

In this vast map of feelings untold,
Every path leads to brave and bold.
With every step, there's a chance to grow,
Exploring the emotions that ebb and flow.

Voices in the Wind

The wind carries secrets untold,
In its whispers, the brave grow bold.
Echoes of laughter, sighs of the past,
Dance on the breeze, a spell they cast.

Rustling leaves share stories anew,
Of dreams and hopes that once flew.
Clouds gather, their messages clear,
In the soft murmurs, we draw near.

From mountains high to valleys low,
Nature's chorus begins to flow.
With every gust, the heart aligns,
To the melody of unseen signs.

Voices beckon from every side,
Inviting us onward, like a tide.
The air vibrates with quiet grace,
As we search for our rightful place.

In unity, the whispers blend,
A symphony that will not end.
We follow the sound, the gentle call,
As the wind weaves stories for all.

Finding the Unseen

Hidden paths in shadows deep,
Where secrets lie and spirits leap.
In silence whispers softly unfold,
Tales of treasures, quietly told.

Beneath the surface, the currents swirl,
A tapestry of life begins to unfurl.
Eyes closed tight, yet visions appear,
In the spaces where doubts disappear.

The night sky twinkles, stars aglow,
Light years away, they silently show.
Yet in their distance, a lesson resides,
In seeking the unseen, the heart abides.

Footsteps echo on forgotten trails,
Tracing the stories where memory pales.
Through the fog, clarity gleams,
As we chase down our wildest dreams.

The unseen waits with arms spread wide,
In every journey, it will abide.
With courage, we dive beyond the known,
Finding magic in the depths we've grown.

Revelations in the Depths

In the deep silence of twilight's embrace,
Lies a treasure, a sacred space.
Beneath the waves, the truth lies.
Revelations bloom, where darkness sighs.

Echoes of thoughts weave through the night,
Shining gently like stars so bright.
What lies buried beneath the surface,
Holds the flames of a divine purpose.

In shadows deep, fears often tread,
Yet wisdom whispers in the ebbing dread.
With every dive, we learn to see,
The beauty that breathes in mystery.

Tides will turn, the tides will teach,
Each wave carries what hearts can reach.
In depths unknown, we find our core,
Emerging stronger than ever before.

Revelations in the depths unfold,
A journey of spirit, brave and bold.
We dive into darkness to find the light,
In the depths of our souls, we take flight.

A Canvas of Hidden Colors

In twilight's embrace, secrets unfold,
Shades of silence, stories untold.
Brush strokes whisper on the quiet air,
A tapestry woven with tender care.

Each hue a heartbeat, each shade a sigh,
Beneath the surface, truths lie.
In the gallery of dreams, colors collide,
In every crevice, the soul's pride.

With every stroke, a memory glows,
Echoes of joy where the wildflower grows.
A splash of rebel, a dash of grace,
A canvas of hidden, a sacred space.

In shadows, the colors begin to speak,
In the quiet corners, emotions peak.
A blend of chaos and calm divine,
In every color, a thread, a line.

This canvas alive, a spell it weaves,
Where hope dances and the heart believes.
In silence, the bright colors dare,
To unveil the world, a joyful prayer.

The Unfolding of Hidden Pages

In the library of whispers, stories call,
Unseen chapters lining the wall.
With every turn, a new world waits,
Life's quiet secrets, inked in fates.

Pages of longing, age-old and wise,
Ink stains of laughter, tears in disguise.
The flutter of pages, a breath of time,
Hiding the rhythm, the pulse, the rhyme.

Beneath the dust, the dreams reside,
Each line a journey, a twist, a tide.
Words woven closely, stitched into night,
Beckoning souls to drink in the light.

A flicker of truth in the margins small,
Echoes of voices from the ancient hall.
In the unfolding, hearts find their way,
Through the pages where shadows play.

Here lies the essence of what we seek,
The unseen threads that bind the meek.
In the sanctuary, old tales rewrite,
The unfolding of pages reveals our light.

Reciting the Language of the Soul

In twilight's hush, the whispers rise,
A symphony sung beneath the skies.
Words like petals, fragile and bright,
Recite the language wrapped in the night.

Each note a dream, softly it flows,
In silence, the melody gently grows.
A dance of spirit, of heart's sweet refrain,
In this sacred space, love's paradox reigns.

The echo of laughter, the sigh of the breeze,
In every vibration, a moment to seize.
Language unspoken, yet understood,
In the rhythm of life, we are all imbued.

A tapestry woven with threads of light,
Harmony painting the dark into bright.
Each verse a heartbeat, a life spun whole,
Reciting the music that dwells in the soul.

In the quiet corners, our spirits embrace,
Each whispered word finds its rightful place.
Together we weave in this celestial dance,
In the language of the soul, we find our chance.

The Dance of Delicate Truths

In the moonlit glow, shadows take flight,
A dance of whispers in the soft night.
Delicate truths, like petals, unfold,
In the embrace of stories, forever bold.

With every twirl, the heart skips a beat,
A rhythm spins where silence meets.
In the gentle sway, we learn to trust,
In the dance of the night, return to dust.

Each tender step reveals what we hide,
In the intricate layers where secrets abide.
The harmony sings through the fragile air,
As delicate truths find courage to share.

With every glance, a spark ignites,
In the dance of the mind, beauty ignites.
Together we leap, unbound, unchained,
In the freedom of movement, wisdom gained.

So let us dance in the soft moon's gaze,
To the rhythm of life, a transient blaze.
In the gentle truth where our souls align,
We find our place, forever entwined.

Portraits of the Spirit

In whispered hues, we paint our dreams,
Each stroke a vision, vibrant schemes.
Faces of laughter, shadows of pain,
Captured in stillness, in joy and in strain.

Eyes that sparkle, stories untold,
Reflections of warmth in moments of cold.
With every glance, a truth we find,
A portrait of spirit, beautifully blind.

Through life's gallery, we wander wide,
Sketches of heartache we hold inside.
A tapestry woven, bright and dim,
The soul's masterpiece, the light and the whim.

With colors of hope and shades of despair,
We carve our legacy, lay our hearts bare.
Each stroke a whisper, a timeless art,
A portrait of spirit, a work of the heart.

Gardens of Reflection

In quiet corners where shadows play,
Petals of thought drift softly away.
Each flower whispers tales of old,
In gardens of reflection, wisdom unfolds.

Under the boughs, where dreams intertwine,
Sunlight dances on leaves, divine.
A tapestry blooming in vibrant hues,
In every petal, a secret muse.

Breezes carry the fragrance of lore,
In the garden, our spirits explore.
Moments of silence, the beauty of pause,
In gardens of reflection, life gives applause.

With every turn, a lesson anew,
In the bloom of the heart, our spirits break through.
Amongst the blossoms, we find our way,
In gardens of reflection, we cherish the day.

Rising from the Ashes

From the embers of pain, we learn to soar,
Each spark a reminder, we are meant for more.
Like phoenixes dancing in the night sky,
We rise from the ashes, bold spirits fly.

Gathering strength from trials endured,
Through shadows and struggles, we have matured.
With wings of resilience, we take to the air,
Rising from ashes, our souls lay bare.

The flames of despair may leave us charred,
Yet from these wounds, we emerge unscarred.
In bright rebirth, new chapters ignite,
From the ashes of darkness, we claim our light.

Through the fire, we shed our past,
With courage ignited, our spirits recast.
Embracing the journey, we conquer the fall,
Rising from ashes, we stand tall.

Navigating Inner Storms

In the depths of chaos, a tempest brews,
Waves crash within, tumultuous views.
Heartbeats echo like thunderous roars,
Navigating storms, we open the doors.

When shadows gather and hope feels small,
We seek the horizon, we hear the call.
Through swirling winds and restless tides,
We find our compass, where courage abides.

With sails of wisdom, we chart our course,
Riding the waves with unyielding force.
Trusting the journey, we'll weather the rain,
Navigating inner storms, we break every chain.

In the heart of the squall, we learn to be strong,
Finding our rhythm, a powerful song.
For in every storm, there's also a calm,
Navigating inner storms, we find our balm.

The Labyrinth of Self

In corridors of thought, I roam,
Finding paths that lead me home.
Each turn reveals the hidden me,
A puzzle crafted by decree.

Mirrors reflect what I have lost,
In shadows deep, I count the cost.
Echoes linger in the air,
Whispers soft, a quiet care.

A flicker of light, a guiding spark,
Illuminates the endless dark.
With every step, I learn to be,
A wanderer in my own decree.

Through twisting paths of joy and pain,
I gather strength to break the chain.
With every breath, I rise anew,
The labyrinth unfolds its view.

At last, I stand and see my core,
The maze dissolves, I seek no more.
In silence, I find my true name,
And love the self that feels no shame.

Songs of the Inner World

In the stillness, melodies play,
Voices whisper through the gray.
Every note, a tale to tell,
In the heart where echoes dwell.

Rhythms dance like fleeting dreams,
Woven through the sunlit beams.
Harmony in every sigh,
Painting wonders in the sky.

Chords that resonate with grace,
Filling every empty space.
The symphony of mind and soul,
In each heartbeat, I am whole.

Rivers flow in vibrant tones,
Carving paths through ancient stones.
Each song a journey, wild and free,
Tracing lines of what could be.

In the quiet, I find my song,
A melody where I belong.
In the chamber of my heart's delight,
The inner world shines oh so bright.

Chasing Shadows of Truth

In the twilight, shadows blend,
Searching truths that never end.
With every step, I seek the light,
In the darkness, shadows fight.

Questions linger, doubts arise,
What is real beneath disguise?
Fleeting glimpses, truths in flight,
Glimmer softly, out of sight.

With every whisper on the breeze,
I chase the truth, my heart appease.
A dance of shadows, light bemused,
In the silence, I am fused.

Guided by the moon's embrace,
Each step unveils a hidden space.
In the chase, I find my plea,
Truth is more than what I see.

As dawn arrives with gentle grace,
Illuminating every face.
The shadows fade, but I remain,
A seeker of the sweet refrain.

Blossoming in Solitude

In quiet corners, petals grow,
Roots entwined beneath the snow.
Solitude, a gentle friend,
Helps the weary heart to mend.

In stillness, I find my voice,
Amidst the noise, I make a choice.
To bloom where nothing else can thrive,
In solitude, I come alive.

Each moment a chance to reflect,
In whispers, secrets I collect.
Nurtured by the sunlit days,
I blossom in so many ways.

As colors burst in soft embrace,
I find my joy, I find my grace.
In every petal, a story told,
Of resilience, brave and bold.

Through solitude, I learn to soar,
Embracing self, I yearn for more.
In the garden of my heart's delight,
I flourish in the morning light.

Chasing the Whisper of Longing

In the hush of twilight's glaze,
Dreams flicker like distant stars.
Hearts beat a quiet phrase,
Yearning to conquer their scars.

Winds sway the leaves in dance,
A melody lost in the night.
Hope stirs with every chance,
To find what feels so right.

Footsteps echo on the shore,
Each wave a tale to tell.
In longing we seek for more,
As hearts weave their silent spell.

Through shadows, whispers leap,
Stories untold, yet near.
We wander, and slowly we keep,
A map drawn by every tear.

In the dawn, longing awakes,
A gentle spark in the day.
New paths, as the heart breaks,
Lead us to love's warm sway.

Redeeming the Roots of My Spirit

From beneath the soil I rise,
Bound by history and grace.
The tales of old never die,
In shadows, I find my place.

Branches stretch toward the blue,
Embracing the sun's golden kiss.
Each leaf tells tales anew,
Of hope, love, and bliss.

The seasons turn with their song,
Nurturing dreams to take flight.
In the heart, I feel so strong,
Reclaiming my inner light.

Through the storm, I stand firm,
Trusting what's deep in my core.
In the roots, I find the term,
To rise and strive for more.

With each breath, I begin,
Harmonizing with my land.
As seeds of joy grow within,
I flourish, I understand.

Shifting Sands of Time

Time flows like a river's glide,
Each moment slips away.
We trust in the changing tide,
As night fades into day.

Footsteps lost in the grains,
Echoes of laughter and tears.
Every joy, every pain,
Carved deep over the years.

The sun sets, a fleeting glance,
Reminding us to cherish now.
In life's unending dance,
We learn to take a bow.

Fleeting time, a whispering breeze,
Guiding us through the unknown.
In its grasp, we seek to seize,
The love that we have grown.

As stars twinkle in the dark,
Lessons cherished in our hearts.
Each heartbeat, a luminous spark,
Where creation never departs.

The Gentle Echo of Rediscovery

In silence, I hear a call,
A voice from deep within.
Whispers soft, a gentle thrall,
Urging me to begin.

Old tales dance in my mind,
Unraveled threads of the past.
With new eyes, I'm defined,
In shadows that quietly cast.

The mirror reflects new light,
Revealing the soul inside.
Every flaw becomes a sight,
A part of love, not pride.

In the garden of the mind,
Flowers bloom, colors bright.
Rediscovery is kind,
Turning darkness into light.

With each step, I reclaim,
The essence of who I am.
Through the echoes, I find flame,
And in that, love's great plan.

Awakening the Dreamer

In the silence of the night,
A spark of hope ignites,
Whispers of the heart arise,
Guiding souls to distant sights.

Through the mist of waking dreams,
The universe softly beams,
Eyes that closed now open wide,
Chasing light in vibrant streams.

Every heartbeat sings a tale,
Of bravery that will not pale,
With the dawn, the shadows fade,
As fears drift like a fragile sail.

Awakening the dreamer's light,
Embracing truth without fright,
In the garden of the mind,
Blooming visions take their flight.

Together we will rise and soar,
To places never seen before,
With each step, a brand new start,
Awakening forevermore.

Beneath the Surface of Time

Beneath the waves of shifting sand,
Lies a story, vast and grand,
Time's whisper echoes low and clear,
In the depths, we understand.

Faded memories drift and glow,
Like the tides that come and go,
Secrets buried, lost in light,
Waiting softly, seeds to sow.

Moments dance in timeless flow,
Like a river's endless show,
Every heartbeat feels the pull,
Of the past, a gentle woe.

In stillness, we shall find the clue,
Beneath the surface, visions due,
Time reveals its tender grace,
Guiding us, forever new.

With each ripple, wisdom calls,
As the ancient water falls,
Embracing all that's been and gone,
We rise up, breaking walls.

The Gentle Revolution

In the dawn of softer dreams,
A revolution quietly beams,
With each voice that dares to rise,
Harmony flows in golden streams.

No loud cries or heavy hands,
Just a heart that understands,
With compassion, we will stand,
Building peace on gentle lands.

Change unfolds like petals wide,
With love as our faithful guide,
In the rhythm of each heartbeat,
A new world will now abide.

Stepping lightly on the Earth,
In the silence, the rebirth,
Together we create the light,
A gentle canvas, filled with worth.

With our steps, we shape the way,
In unity, we choose to stay,
Through the whispers of the soul,
The gentle revolution sways.

The Silent Awakening

In the hush of twilight's gleam,
Awakens calm within the dream,
Beneath the stars, all souls unite,
In stillness, life begins to teem.

A breath taken, deeply felt,
Where silence and spirit melt,
Each moment holds a promise bright,
In the calm, new stories are dealt.

A gentle touch ignites the flame,
In every heart, a whispered name,
From shadows to the radiant light,
We rise up, never the same.

Through the stillness, truths arise,
In the quiet, wisdom lies,
As the world keeps turning on,
In silence, all fear dies.

The awakening, soft and clear,
Embraces what we hold so dear,
In the gentle flow of time,
We find forever resting here.

The Unfolding Story

In whispers soft, the tale begins,
Each page turned, the heart now spins.
A dance of words, both sweet and bold,
The ink flows freely, stories told.

Woven dreams in twilight's glow,
Secrets shared, yet few may know.
A canvas bright, with colors true,
Life's vibrant hues, old and new.

With every chapter, lessons learned,
Paths crossed and fires burned.
A journey traced through time and space,
In every line, a warm embrace.

Through laughter, tears, and moments dear,
The story grows, year by year.
A tapestry of hopes and fears,
Crafted gently, through the years.

As dawn breaks light on pages wide,
The author smiles with heart and pride.
For every ending sparks a start,
The unfolding story, a work of art.

A Journey to the Core

Beneath the surface, treasures lie,
Where echoes dwell and dreams can fly.
A quest unfolds in shadows deep,
Awakening the soul from sleep.

With every step, the ground gives way,
Revealing truths that softly sway.
The heart's compass leads us true,
To depths unknown, yet ever new.

Each layer pulled, like a soft veil,
Secrets waiting, soft as a trail.
The pulse of earth, a steady beat,
Guiding us where worlds do meet.

Through darkness deep and caverns cold,
The fire within begins to unfold.
With courage found and spirits bold,
We seek the stories yet untold.

The journey maps the inner self,
A treasure hunt, not gold or wealth.
In every heartbeat, lessons soar,
In finding self, we journey more.

When Night Meets Dawn

In twilight's hush, the stars ignite,
A canvas painted with soft light.
Whispers dance on the evening air,
As day gives way, the night lays bare.

A moment stretched, suspended time,
The world transforms, an endless mime.
In shadows deep, the dreams take flight,
When all is calm, and hearts feel light.

The horizon blushes, fiery glow,
As secrets shared in the night's flow.
In silent promise, the dawn prepares,
To brush the world with gentle cares.

A symphony of night and day,
In harmony, they softly play.
With every breath, a new refrain,
Life's cycles dance through joy and pain.

As night retreats, the sun ascends,
The cycle spins, the journey bends.
In perfect balance, life will shine,
When night meets dawn, love's pure design.

Charting Unwritten Waters

Upon the waves, we set our sail,
With dreams afloat, we will not fail.
Each ripple tells a tale untold,
Of voyages grand, brave and bold.

The compass spins, yet guides us still,
Through storms that test the heart and will.
In every wave, a lesson learned,
As stars above remind, we yearned.

The horizon calls with whispered tales,
Of distant lands and mystic trails.
With open hearts, we face the tide,
In unknown realms, together abide.

The charts await, with ink yet dry,
As courage swells, we learn to fly.
Each splash a note in nature's song,
A melody where we belong.

Through uncharted realms, our spirits soar,
With every breath, we seek for more.
In the quiet depths, new dreams awaken,
Charting waters, never forsaken.

In the Embrace of Stillness

In the quiet woods we dwell,
Whispers of nature's gentle spell.
A moment's peace, a breath of air,
Time stands still, free from care.

Sunlight dapples through the trees,
Softly swaying with the breeze.
Colors blend in vibrant hues,
Nature's canvas, full of views.

Birds serenade the morning light,
Their melodies take to the height.
Each note a thread in the song,
In the stillness, we belong.

Rivers flow without a sound,
In their depths, truths are found.
Reflections dance, a fleeting glance,
A moment's peace, a state of trance.

As twilight falls, the stars appear,
In their glow, we have no fear.
In stillness, hearts beat as one,
A quiet joy when day is done.

The Tapestry of Us

Threads of laughter, woven tight,
Colors bright in the fading light.
Each moment shared, a stitch of grace,
Together we find our sacred space.

From whispered secrets to dreams that soar,
In this tapestry, we explore.
Hand in hand, we weave our tale,
With every heartbeat, we shall not fail.

Patterns change, yet remain true,
Every shade reflects me and you.
Through the storms and sunny days,
Our story glimmers in myriad ways.

Every knot a challenge faced,
Every tear a memory laced.
In the fabric of our lives so sweet,
Our hearts entwined, a rhythmic beat.

Moments gathered, rich and rare,
In the tapestry, love's warmth is there.
Together we stand, forever entwined,
In this masterpiece, our souls aligned.

Echoes of Forgotten Songs

In shadowed halls, the echoes call,
Soft whispers bounce off crumbling walls.
Forgotten melodies drift and sway,
Carried on the winds of yesterday.

Notes of laughter, tinged with tears,
Resonate through the passing years.
Each chord a memory held so tight,
Illuminating the depths of night.

Songs of lovers, brave and bold,
Stories of warmth in the winter's cold.
Each harmony seeks to revive,
The whispers of those who once thrived.

Crackled records, spinning slow,
In the silence, we still know.
Ghostly echoes of dreams long gone,
In our hearts, they still live on.

Melodies born from the twilight,
In shadows deep, they dance in flight.
Each note a thread, a timeless claim,
Binding souls in love's sweet name.

Navigating the Inner Seas

In depths unseen, the waters flow,
Currents shift, and feelings grow.
Charting paths through waves of thought,
Finding solace in battles fought.

Sailing ships of dreams set free,
Guided by stars, we seek to see.
Each wave a question, a call to be,
Navigating through the ageless sea.

Storms may rise, skies turn gray,
Yet in our hearts, we'll find our way.
Anchors dropped in tranquil bays,
Moments cherished, time betrays.

The compass spins, yet still we roam,
In our journey, find our home.
Charted maps of joy and pain,
We'll emerge whole from every strain.

As tides retreat, new shores appear,
With every wave, we shed our fear.
In the abyss, light will gleam,
Navigating life, we find our dream.

The Voice in Silence

In shadows deep, whispers drift,
A quiet song, a gentle gift.
In silent nights, the heart will speak,
In stillness find the words we seek.

Beneath the stars, a truth unfolds,
In hushed moments, a tale is told.
The echo of thoughts, soft yet clear,
In the silence, we draw near.

A longing found in quiet grace,
Each pause, a sacred space.
In listening deep, we truly hear,
The voice that calms our every fear.

In solitude, we learn to trust,
The silent whispers, a must.
For in the quiet, we find our way,
The voice in silence leads the day.

So cherish moments where silence reigns,
For in that stillness, peace remains.
Let the whispers guide your flight,
In the heart of the night.

Where the Dreams Reside

Beyond the hills, where wishes soar,
In realms of wonder, evermore.
A tapestry of hopes unspun,
Where heartbeats echo, dreams begun.

In twilight hours, swirls of light,
Paint visions bold upon the night.
With every star, a dream takes flight,
In the quiet, we seek the bright.

Amidst the clouds, our spirits fly,
Painting futures in the sky.
Where laughter dances, joy abides,
In these corners, love resides.

The heart remembers what it seeks,
In whispered winds, the soul speaks.
Through shadows soft, dreams will confide,
In cherished whispers, we abide.

So journey forth, let courage guide,
To that place where dreams reside.
In the magic of the night,
Find treasures bold, take your flight.

Unveiling Hidden Layers

Beneath the surface, stories dwell,
With every glance, a tale to tell.
In silence wrapped, secrets take form,
Unveiling life, a quiet storm.

Each layer shed, like autumn leaves,
Revealing truths the heart believes.
Through gentle touch, we start to see,
The beauty held in mystery.

In solitude, reflections rise,
Hidden depths, a sweet surprise.
With every breath, the soul ignites,
Unveiling starry, endless nights.

So peel away the masks we wear,
In honesty, let love lay bare.
Through open hearts, we break the chain,
Unveiling joy from every pain.

For in the layers, life's embrace,
We find each other, find our place.
In every truth, a spark ignites,
Unveiling dreams in endless nights.

Essence of Understanding

In tender moments, we connect,
The essence of love we can detect.
With every word, a bridge we build,
The heart's vast ocean, gently filled.

Through eyes that see beyond the veil,
In silence shared, we tell our tale.
With empathy, we break the walls,
In understanding, true love calls.

Each story shared, a lesson learned,
For in this dance, respect is earned.
Through hearts united, hearts in tune,
We find our light beneath the moon.

With gentle hands, we heal the scars,
In this journey, we reach the stars.
For in each soul, a world unfolds,
The essence of understanding holds.

So grasp the threads that weave us near,
In love and kindness, hold it dear.
In every heartbeat, in every sigh,
The essence of life will never die.

Awakening Within

In morning's light, I rise anew,
The whispers call, a song so true.
Within the heart, a spark ignites,
As dreams unfold in gentle flights.

The shadows dance, the silence breaks,
With every breath, a choice I make.
The journey stirs, a path revealed,
In stillness found, my fate is sealed.

The world around begins to fade,
In this embrace, no masquerade.
I touch the void, where fears reside,
And find the strength I've often denied.

The mirror shows the soul's true hue,
Reflecting back a life so new.
With open arms, I welcome change,
In this bold dance, I rearrange.

Awakening brings a deeper sight,
Through darkest nights, I seek the light.
In every tear, a lesson learned,
Each moment cherished, brightly burned.

Shadows of Discovery

In twilight's glow, the shadows play,
Revealing truths that hide away.
Each whispered thought, a secret shared,
In quiet corners, we've all dared.

The labyrinth of mind unfolds,
With winding paths and stories told.
We seek the light, yet fear the dark,
For in its depth, we find the spark.

Echoes linger, haunting yet sweet,
In solitude, the heart will meet.
Each memory, a treasure chest,
Where fragments lie, yearning for rest.

Through shadows cast, we learn to see,
The beauty in our fragility.
With every step, the heartbeats guide,
In the dance of life, we must abide.

With courage found in gentle sighs,
Through tangled webs, the spirit flies.
The shadows fade, revealing grace,
In every challenge, we find our place.

Echoes of the Soul

In silence deep, the echoes rise,
A symphony that never lies.
Each heartbeat sways, each breath a song,
In timeless dance, we all belong.

Moments fade, yet shadows stay,
Like whispers carried far away.
Through corridors of memory,
We find the truth, our destiny.

In winds that howl, in softest breeze,
The soul speaks out, it seeks to please.
In every laugh, in every tear,
The echoes call, forever near.

With open arms, we gather near,
Embracing love, dispelling fear.
The tapestry, a vivid thread,
In every color, life is spread.

Through troubled times, we find a way,
In darkest nights, we seek the day.
The echoes linger, soft and bold,
A story waits, waiting to be told.

Journey to the Mirror

I stand before the glass so clear,
Reflections whisper, calm my fear.
In every crack, a tale unfolds,
Of dreams once lost and love retold.

The journey starts with each small step,
A forward glance, no promise kept.
Through every trial, we learn to grow,
In the stillness, our truths we sow.

The mirror laughs, it knows my name,
In laughter shared, I feel no shame.
With open heart, I gaze within,
To find the light where hope begins.

Each line a story, chiseled deep,
In every sorrow, joy to keep.
The journey shapes, as night meets dawn,
In every ending, new light is born.

And so I walk this path of light,
Embracing shadows, holding tight.
The mirror's truth, a lasting friend,
In this journey, I'll never end.

Embracing the Echoes

Whispers float on twilight's breath,
Memories dance in shadows' depth.
Each ripple calls, a soft refrain,
Echoing love, joy, and pain.

Hearts entwined in silent song,
Time's passage feels both right and wrong.
Through valleys deep, our spirits soar,
In every echo, we seek more.

Footsteps lead to unseen trails,
Laughter weaves where silence fails.
In every sound, a story lives,
In every pause, the heart forgives.

Nature sings in harmonies bright,
Day meets dusk, a beautiful sight.
We embrace what whispers near,
In echoes, love, we hold dear.

As stars awaken, dreams take flight,
Guided softly by the night.
In every echo, a chance to find,
The love that lingers, intertwined.

The Hidden Lantern

In quiet corners, shadows hide,
A flicker glows, the soul's true guide.
Banished fears, ignited flame,
In darkened paths, we stake our claim.

Secrets whispered in twilight's glow,
A lantern reveals what we must know.
Hope unfurls amidst despair,
Lighting journeys, everywhere.

Beneath the stars, hearts open wide,
Beams of truth we no longer bide.
The hidden lantern's gentle spark,
Brings forth dreams to light the dark.

Through winding roads and whispered pleas,
We chase the light, find inner peace.
Each flicker holds a purpose clear,
In every glow, our path draws near.

So let it shine, the lantern bright,
Guiding us through the endless night.
In hidden depths, we start to see,
The light inside, setting us free.

Solstice of Self

In the stillness of summer's peak,
We pause to find the words we speak.
Reflections dance in golden rays,
A journey marked by lengthening days.

The sun bestows a gentle gift,
As shadows fade, our spirits lift.
In nature's heartbeat, we embrace,
The essence of our sacred space.

Through open fields, we roam and soar,
Understanding ourselves, we explore.
Each moment shines, a chance to grow,
In the solstice light, our true selves glow.

As twilight whispers, dreams unfold,
The stories that our hearts have told.
With every breath, we weave anew,
A tapestry of hope and truth.

Celebrate this dance of time,
Linking our souls with the divine.
In the solstice of self, we find,
A journey shared, forever intertwined.

In the Garden of Secrets

A garden grows where shadows play,
Whispers weave through night and day.
In petals soft, the secrets rest,
A world of wonder, deeply blessed.

Among the blooms, a tale unfolds,
Of hidden dreams and hearts of gold.
Each blossom holds a wish untold,
In fragrant air, life's truths unfold.

With gentle hands, we tend the soil,
Nurturing moments, free of toil.
In every leaf, a story speaks,
In every root, the essence seeks.

The moonlight bathes the garden bright,
As stars emerge to share their light.
In whispered winds, our hopes reside,
In this sanctuary, we confide.

Let time stand still in this embrace,
Among the secrets, we find grace.
In the garden flourishes our heart,
In every part, love's gentle art.

Illuminating the Inner Landscape

In twilight's grasp, shadows dance,
Whispers of dreams in a fleeting trance.
Stars flicker softly, secrets engage,
Painting the heart in hues of the sage.

Beneath the surface, tides ebb and flow,
Silent rivers of feelings grow.
Each thought a petal, fragile yet bold,
Revealing mysteries quietly told.

Caverns of memory, dark yet bright,
Echo the journeys that shape our night.
With every heartbeat, the canvas expands,
Coloring life with invisible hands.

Through valleys of doubt, we often roam,
Searching for a place we can call home.
Illuminated paths merge and diverge,
Fortifying spirits as they emerge.

In the depths of self, there lies a flame,
A beacon of hope, warm and untamed.
With gentle resolve, we find our way,
Illuminated souls, come what may.

Fragments of the Untold Story

In whispered tones, the past implores,
Fragments of tales behind closed doors.
Scattered like leaves on an autumn trail,
Each a reminder of joy and travail.

Silent moments hold the weight of time,
Shadows of truth in their silent climb.
A photograph faded, a glance misplaced,
Suggests the love that was once embraced.

Echoes of laughter, soft as a sigh,
Memories linger, refusing to die.
In the creases of pages, stories reside,
Layers of lives that we sometimes hide.

A tapestry woven with threads of fate,
Each stitch a heartbeat, every knot innate.
Untold epics in the silence thrive,
Yearning for voices that keep them alive.

Dance with the ghosts of what could have been,
In the fragments, the heart can begin.
To weave the narrative, to start anew,
Unfolding the shadows in radiant hue.

An Exploration of Forgotten Paths

Along the edges where wildflowers bloom,
Lies a path overgrown in nature's loom.
Steps softly taken on unmarked trails,
Whispers of stories carried by gales.

Fern-covered stones tell of footsteps past,
Secrets entangled in shadows cast.
Nature's embrace holds the weight of dreams,
Each bend a reminder that nothing's as it seems.

In the hollows, the echoes of song,
Call forth the spirits of what once belonged.
Every turn reveals a treasure to find,
A glimpse of the heart intertwined with the mind.

Cracked earth and sprouting roots intertwine,
A symphony played where the lost align.
In the stillness, a moment to breathe,
Embracing the journeys that make us believe.

As daylight fades, and shadows embrace,
We wander these paths, seeking solace.
In unknown realms, we learn to let go,
Exploring the truth in the wild's gentle flow.

The Quiet Unraveling

In the silence of night, threads come undone,
Emotions like rivers, they flow one by one.
Whispers of truths, softly they sigh,
While the heart learns to question the why.

Fleeting reflections dance in the dark,
Echoes of parts that once held a spark.
The fabric of self begins to divide,
Revealing the layers we often hide.

As shadows retreat and dawn starts to wake,
A gentle reminder, the path we must take.
In the quiet, we find what was lost,
A journey through all that we feared would cost.

Moments of clarity break through the haze,
Casting new light on forgotten ways.
In unraveling threads, we find our own song,
Believing in places where we all belong.

Through quiet reflections and tender embrace,
We gather the scattered with hope and grace.
With every unravel, a new story spins,
The quiet rebirth of the soul that begins.

The Awakening of the Inner Compass

In silence deep, the heart does call,
A whispering guide, it beckons all.
To paths untread, our feet must stray,
Embrace the dawn, light leads the way.

Through shadows cast, a truth unfolds,
In every heartbeat, courage molds.
With every breath, the soul will rise,
A compass formed in gleaming skies.

Awakening dreams, they soar and glide,
An inner light, our steadfast guide.
With every step, our spirits dance,
In this embrace, we find our chance.

The gentle winds, they share our tale,
Through storms and sun, we will prevail.
Together bound, in fate's sweet flow,
The compass found, we learn to grow.

As morning breaks, the shadows flee,
With open hearts, we start to see.
In quietude, we find our song,
The awakening breath, where we belong.

Harvesting the Seeds of Understanding

In fertile ground, we plant the thought,
With gentle care, the lessons sought.
Time waters dreams, with patience rare,
From seeds of doubt, new blooms declare.

Each moment spent, a chance to learn,
In every heart, a fire we burn.
Together we weave the threads of fate,
Harvesting hope, before it's late.

The fields of wisdom, vast and wide,
We gather truth, with hearts as guide.
Through trials faced, and shadows cast,
The seeds of trust grow strong and last.

In bonds we forge, new paths we find,
Hand in hand, our spirits entwined.
With open minds, we take the leap,
The harvest blooms, our souls to keep.

As seasons change, the cycle turns,
Each lesson learned, a light that burns.
With grateful hearts, we celebrate,
In unity, we cultivate.

The Spark Before the Flame

In darkness deep, a spark ignites,
A flicker soft, within the nights.
It swells with hope, a promise made,
To conquer fears, the plans we laid.

With whispered dreams, the future gleams,
A tender glow, from heart's own beams.
Before the flame, we pause and breathe,
In quiet moments, we believe.

Each little spark, a universe,
Of thoughts that dance, and hearts immersed.
With every thought, a fire unfurls,
In mind's embrace, a world of whirls.

As passion's heat begins to rise,
Creation blooms beneath the skies.
The spark transforms, a blaze takes flight,
Illuminating the dark of night.

With focused hearts, our journey starts,
The flame ignited, light imparts.
Together we forge our destinies,
From sparks to flames, we'll ride the breeze.

Eclipsed Thoughts and Stars Reborn

In solitude, the mind takes flight,
Eclipsed thoughts roam in the night.
A veil is drawn, yet hope persists,
In shadows deep, new dreams exist.

Through cosmic dance, the stars will shine,
Rebirthed from depths, the light divine.
We chase the echoes of what's real,
In every heart, the wounds can heal.

As thoughts unite, a chorus sings,
A tapestry of endless wings.
In every loss, a gain is found,
The stars reborn, in wholeness bound.

As eclipsed minds seek out the dawn,
In unity, the blind spots drawn.
We rise anew, with strength bestowed,
In shadows cast, our stories flowed.

The universe whispers, soft and clear,
From dark to light, we have no fear.
With every star, a guide we know,
Eclipsed thoughts fade, as brilliance grows.

The Path to Clarity

In shadows deep, the mind will roam,
Seeking light, a place called home.
With every step, the fog will lift,
Revealing truths, a precious gift.

The whispers strong, they guide the way,
Through tangled thoughts, a brighter day.
Embrace the shift, the inward quest,
A journey long, but for the best.

Mistakes laid bare, fears left behind,
With open heart, a growing mind.
Each lesson learned, a stone we'll lay,
To pave the road, come what may.

The streams of doubt may run so wide,
Yet courage grows when fear subsides.
A clearer view, as skies unfold,
The path ahead, a tale retold.

In time we'll find the truth so bright,
Our hearts ablaze, ignited light.
With every breath, we claim the day,
On this path, we find our way.

Dance of Self-Discovery

In silent rooms, the heart does weave,
A tapestry, of dreams we believe.
With every beat, a rhythm found,
A dance of self, unbroken ground.

Spinning round, the shadows fade,
In movements raw, our fears displayed.
We twirl to songs of ancient days,
Where strength we find in gentle ways.

Each step we take, a choice in grace,
Unveiling lines upon our face.
With every fall, a lesson learned,
A soul ignites, a passion burned.

In laughter shared, in tears embraced,
The dance continues, time can't erase.
We celebrate what makes us whole,
In every beat, we find our soul.

With open arms, we sway and spin,
The dance of life, let joy begin.
United here, in this grand trance,
We find ourselves in every glance.

Beneath the Surface

The ocean's calm, a mirror's gaze,
Beneath the waves, a hidden maze.
With depths unknown, stories untold,
Each current flows, a world of gold.

Coral dreams in colors bright,
In shadows deep, hidden from light.
Fish dart through, like thoughts in flight,
A symphony played, day and night.

The weight of silence, pulled below,
In whispered tides, the secrets flow.
What lurks beneath, we long to see,
The depths of heart, the soul set free.

In quiet hours, reflections bloom,
We gladly face the inner gloom.
With courage, we explore each wave,
To find the strength that makes us brave.

So dive right in, make waves anew,
Beneath the surface, find the true.
In depths we learn, in darkness shine,
A treasure waits, forever mine.

Mosaic of Identity

Each fragment shines, a story clear,
In shades of love, in hues of fear.
We stitch together, piece by piece,
A masterpiece that will not cease.

In laughter's echo, in silence sweet,
The mosaic grows beneath our feet.
With colors bold, and textures rough,
In every shard, we find the tough.

The scars we wear, a tale of grace,
In every break, a sacred space.
Blending paths, we weave and twine,
A dance of souls, forever align.

With every choice, the patterns shift,
A unique blend, a timeless gift.
In every heart, a piece we share,
A world of voices, rich and rare.

So celebrate the bits we hold,
In unity, the stories told.
A mosaic bright, our spirits soar,
Together as one, forevermore.

Pathways of the Heart

In the quiet of the night,
Whispers echo soft and light.
Each step taken, brave and bold,
Leads to stories yet untold.

In the garden where dreams bloom,
Love finds space to gently loom.
Every heartbeat, every sigh,
Carves the paths where hopes can fly.

Through the valleys, up the hills,
Every journey, new heart thrills.
With each twist, the spirit grows,
Finding where true essence flows.

As the sunlight starts to fade,
Shadows dance in lovely braid.
In this moment, truth appears,
Mapping dreams through joys and fears.

When the dawn begins to break,
Embracing all the steps we take.
Pathways cross, and bonds ignite,
Within our hearts, eternal light.

Voices Beneath the Stars

In the stillness of the night,
Voices whisper, songs take flight.
Guided by the moon's soft glow,
Stars reveal what hearts should know.

Lullabies of ages past,
Stories woven, shadows cast.
Echoes float on midnight air,
Every dream, a jewel rare.

In the dance of constellations,
Each voice sings of new temptations.
Together, we find our place,
Wrapped in time's warm, sweet embrace.

Underneath the cosmic quilt,
Hearts entwined, the fears are stilled.
With each note, we come alive,
In this symphony, we strive.

As dawn approaches with its hue,
Voices fade but dreams renew.
Beneath the stars, we shall remain,
Bound by love, through joy and pain.

The Silent Symphony

In the hush of twilight's glow,
Softest sounds begin to flow.
Strings of silence gently play,
Crafting night from hues of day.

Notes of starlight, cool and clear,
Make the unseen songs appear.
In the resonance of the breeze,
Whispers dance among the trees.

Every heartbeat, every pause,
Adds to nature's grand applause.
In the quiet, truth unfolds,
Turning whispers into gold.

As the shadows start to blend,
Harmony that knows no end.
Lost in moments rich and deep,
In this silence, we shall leap.

With the dawn, the symphony fades,
But within us, music stays.
Every breath a note so pure,
In our hearts, the tune endures.

Mirroring the Cosmos

In the depths of night, we gaze,
Reflections set the heart ablaze.
Galaxies within our mind,
Searching for the love we find.

Stars align to share their truth,
Fragments of a timeless youth.
Every sparkle, every spark,
Guides us through the endless dark.

In the dance of planets' sway,
We discover our own way.
Embracing all that we can be,
In the vastness, we are free.

Constellations drawn so bright,
Painting dreams in the night light.
Each reflection, a new start,
Mirroring the cosmic heart.

As the dawn ignites the sky,
Echoes of the night pass by.
In our souls, the stars still gleam,
Living on in every dream.

The Wind's Whisper

The breeze speaks softly through the trees,
Carrying secrets across the seas.
It rustles leaves and sways the grass,
In gentle tones, the moments pass.

Whispers of past in every swirl,
Stories unfurl, like ribbons whirl.
A dance of nature, light and free,
The wind's sweet song calls out to me.

A sigh of change, a hint of rain,
It comforts hearts that ache with pain.
A fleeting glance, a fleeting sound,
In its embrace, I am unbound.

Through valleys low and mountains high,
The wind will carry dreams to sky.
With every gust, a promise made,
In whispered tones, my fears will fade.

In twilight's glow, I pause to hear,
The secrets that the night holds dear.
The wind's soft breath, a lullaby,
In its embrace, I learn to fly.

Stones in My Path

With every step, a stone I find,
A memory that lingers, unkind.
They shape my journey, rough and tough,
Each pebble whispers, life is rough.

Some are sharp, they cut the feet,
While others lie in soft retreat.
They teach me strength, they teach me grace,
In every stumble, I find my place.

A mountain made of all my fears,
Heavy burdens, weighted years.
Yet if I pause and look around,
I see the beauty that I've found.

These stones remind me of my might,
To rise again, to seek the light.
In every crack, there blooms a flower,
Resilience thrives in darkest hour.

I gather stones, I wear them proud,
Each one a tale, a lesson loud.
Though paths may twist and turn away,
I cherish stones, come what may.

Heartbeats of Awareness

In silent moments, I can feel,
The rhythm of my heart's appeal.
Each beat a pulse, a calling strong,
In stillness, I find where I belong.

Awareness wraps like morning light,
A gentle nudge that feels so right.
I breathe in deep, the world around,
In awareness, my peace is found.

The flutter of wings, the sigh of trees,
Nature whispers in the breeze.
Each heartbeat syncs with life's own flow,
Connection deep, the more I know.

I listen close, to joy and pain,
The tapestry of love's refrain.
In every strike, a chance to grow,
Amidst the tides, I let it show.

The heartbeat of the earth, alive,
In rhythm shared, we all survive.
With every pulse, I learn to see,
The beauty in our unity.

In Between Worlds

In shadows cast and whispers lost,
I tread the line, between two coasts.
A bridge of dreams, a veil so thin,
In between worlds, I seek within.

Here space and time begin to blend,
Where past and future softly mend.
I dance with echoes, laugh and cry,
In this sacred space, I fly.

The touch of dawn, the kiss of night,
I find my place in the fading light.
With every heartbeat, I take my stand,
A wanderer in both sea and sand.

The voices call, yet softly fade,
In between, I am unafraid.
For here I weave the stories spun,
A tapestry, where all is one.

In stillness, I embrace the now,
To all I've seen, I humbly bow.
In between worlds, my soul takes flight,
Forever seeking, chasing light.

Crucible of Transformation

Through trials we rise, our spirits ignite,
In shadows we find, our will is the light.
Forged in the fire, our true selves emerge,
From ashes of doubt, we gather the surge.

With every heartbeat, the past we embrace,
In moments of stillness, we find our own pace.
Like steel tempered strong, we learn to be brave,
In the crucible's hold, our souls become wave.

Each lesson carved deep, the scars we all wear,
A treasure of strength, in every despair.
Transformation unique, in pain there's a gift,
Through the storm we traverse, our spirits will lift.

In unity formed, we learn to be whole,
As petals unfold, revealing the soul.
With courage as compass, we venture unknown,
And in this great journey, our light is our own.

The cycle of life in colors so bright,
Awakens the heart to embrace the new light.
In the crucible's warmth, we grow and we change,
Life's magic unfolds, in moments so strange.

The Heart's Odyssey

Waves crash on shores, where dreams come to rest,
In the depths of the night, the heart beats its quest.
With whispers of love, it sails on the breeze,
Through valleys of sorrow, it finds its own ease.

Each glance in the dark, a spark to ignite,
With the flicker of hope, we're drawn to the light.
The journey is long, but the path is ours,
In the quiet of dawn, we reach for the stars.

The map of our souls, etched with joy and with pain,
Guides us through storms, through sunshine and rain.
The tides pull and push, yet we learn to be free,
With love as the anchor, we sail through the sea.

Through laughter and tears, the heart's story flows,
In gardens of grace, the beauty still grows.
With every new turn, a lesson unfolds,
As moments become chapters, our destiny molds.

In the dance of the night, hearts beat as one,
United in strength, till the journey is done.
With open minds and arms, we embrace what may,
For the heart's odyssey leads us this way.

Sketches of Freedom

On blank canvases, we color the sky,
With strokes of ambition, our spirits can fly.
Each dream a bold line, each hope a bright hue,
In sketches of freedom, our essence shines through.

We draw with conviction, our minds set ablaze,
In the tapestry woven, we find new ways.
The chains of the past, we shatter and break,
With courage as colors, we boldly partake.

The voices that echo, a symphony grand,
In the chorus of change, we take a stand.
Each breath a brushstroke, defining our fate,
With hearts unconfined, we refuse to wait.

In moments of silence, our visions take flight,
In the sketches of life, we dare to ignite.
With every new dawn, our stories unfold,
In the art of existence, our truth is retold.

As we wander through time, in colors divine,
Our spirits dance free, in rhythm and rhyme.
Through sketches of freedom, we find our true call,
In the masterpiece shared, there is space for us all.

Bursts of Clarity

In chaotic moments, a stillness will bloom,
Amidst the confusion, we break through the gloom.
Like lightning in dark, a flash of insight,
Bursts of clarity ignite the sweet night.

Each thought like a star, shines bright in the haze,
Illuminating paths through the thickest of maze.
With whispers of truth, we uncover the real,
In bursts of clarity, our hearts start to heal.

Embrace the unknown, let go of the fears,
In the quiet of spaces, our vision appears.
With courage to speak the words that we feel,
We break through the chains, our spirits unveil.

With every new dawn, new visions arise,
In the light of the morning, our dreams touch the skies.
Through storms and through calm, we find our own way,
In bursts of clarity, we transform the day.

Let echoes resound, let the laughter be heard,
In moments of truth, our souls are assured.
With wisdom as guide, we navigate, see,
In bursts of clarity, we finally be free.

Rediscovering the Echo Within

In the silence, whispers call,
A hidden voice, it speaks to all.
With every heartbeat, a sign unfolds,
A tale of dreams, waiting to be told.

Through shadows deep, the journey wends,
Finding strength where the spirit bends.
Each step a revelation gained,
In the echo, no longer restrained.

Waves of doubt crash and roar,
Yet within lies an open door.
Embracing the truth that we once knew,
Rediscovering the strength to renew.

In stillness, the heart takes flight,
A beacon shining, pure and bright.
The echo within, a guiding star,
Leading us back to who we are.

In every breath, we find our place,
In every moment, a tender embrace.
The echo whispers, soft and sweet,
A melody of life, a rhythmic beat.

Through the journey, we learn to sing,
Embracing the joy that freedom brings.
The echo within, forever our guide,
In the heart's vast ocean, where secrets reside.

Shattered Mirrors and New Reflections

In the shards of glass, we see the light,
Fragments of dreams scattered in sight.
Each piece a story, a thread to weave,
Of hope and heartache, we dare to believe.

With every crack, a chance to mend,
To rediscover the truth we defend.
In brokenness, beauty finds its way,
A tapestry woven from shadows and clay.

New reflections emerge from the pain,
In the depths of sorrow, love does reign.
Embracing the flaws, we find our grace,
In shattered mirrors, we retake our place.

With courage, we face what once was lost,
Understanding the price we sometimes cost.
New visions rise, vibrant and bold,
In the pieces, stories yet untold.

Together we stand, hearts intertwined,
Finding strength in being maligned.
Shattered mirrors, a canvas anew,
Reflecting the beauty that's always true.

Through the chaos, we learn to shine,
In every crack, a radiant line.
Shattered mirrors, new paths to tread,
In newfound light, our spirits are fed.

Whispers of the Forgotten

In the twilight, shadows softly creep,
Echoes of memories, buried deep.
Whispers flutter like leaves in the breeze,
Calling to souls with subtle ease.

Hidden tales linger in the air,
Glimpses of moments, tender and rare.
A sigh from the past, a gentle refrain,
In the silence, a sweet panama remains.

Embracing the echoes of who we were,
Resonating softly, like a heartbeat's stir.
Whispers of the forgotten, faint yet clear,
Drawing us closer, dispelling our fear.

In the stillness, the heart can hear,
Lost memories, drawing near.
In every whisper, a lesson calling,
In the depths of silence, we're never falling.

As we journey through the ebb and flow,
The whispers lead us, gently they show.
With open hearts, we start to find,
The beauty woven in the strands of time.

In soft murmurs, the past will dance,
Guiding our steps with every chance.
Whispers of the forgotten, sweet and wise,
Awakening the spirit, helping us rise.

The Odyssey of Self-Awareness

Upon the sea of thoughts we sail,
With courage as our hearty trail.
Waves of doubt crashing strong,
Yet in our hearts, we hear the song.

Navigating through tempestuous nights,
The compass turned to inner sights.
Each stormy trial, a lesson bold,
Mapping the journey within our souls.

The horizon glows with the dawn's embrace,
Illuminating shadows we must face.
In still waters, truths come to view,
The odyssey leads us back to the true.

With every ripple, we learn to see,
The depth of our being, wild and free.
Unraveling layers, unveiling light,
In the dance of awareness, futures ignite.

Through valleys deep and mountains high,
Self-awareness teaches us to fly.
Embracing the journey, we find our way,
In the odyssey, our spirits sway.

The map is drawn with moments shared,
Each heartbeat a step, gently bared.
In the odyssey of self, we are reborn,
Awakening strength by love's purest form.

Labyrinth of the Heart

In corridors of dreams we stroll,
Winding paths that echo whole.
Each twist unveils a hidden part,
A maze that dwells within the heart.

Whispers linger in the air,
Secrets woven with utmost care.
Though shadows dance with fleeting light,
Hope guides us through the darkest night.

Every turn reveals a choice,
Silent fears and longing voice.
In this labyrinth, we will find,
Connections forged, hearts intertwined.

Lost and found, we brave the night,
Each step forward, pure delight.
With every heartbeat, trust takes flight,
Leading us towards the light.

In the depths where feelings churn,
With every lesson, we shall learn.
Through labyrinth's twists, love imparts,
The beauty hidden in our hearts.

Embracing the Authentic

Beneath the mask, the truth does lie,
A soul that yearns to touch the sky.
With every flaw, a story blooms,
In the silence, courage looms.

We gather scars like precious jewels,
In the depths, we break the rules.
Taking steps, we shed the guise,
In this journey, we arise.

Authenticity, our guiding star,
No longer bound, we've come so far.
With open hearts, we dare to dance,
Embracing life's wild romance.

Each voice, a note in harmony,
A melody unique and free.
Together we create the sound,
In authenticity, love is found.

Let not the fear of judgment weigh,
For in our truth, we find our way.
Unmasked and brave, we shine so bright,
Embracing all, we claim our life.

Sketches of the Soul

In colors bold, the heart takes flight,
Each stroke a whisper of delight.
Canvas wide, the stories flow,
Sketches born from depths we know.

Lines entwined, a dance of fate,
A journey cherished, love innate.
With each impression, time stands still,
Revealing all the dreams we fulfill.

Textures soft, the feelings blend,
Artistry in every bend.
Through vibrant hues, the soul finds peace,
As echoes of our hearts release.

Golden sunsets, midnight hues,
Every shade a chance to choose.
In this gallery, we find our place,
Sketching memories, love's embrace.

On this canvas, we leave our mark,
With every heartbeat, leave a spark.
These sketches tell a tale so true,
Of vibrant hearts and skies so blue.

Footprints on the Heart

In the sands of time, we tread so light,
Each footprint tells of love's pure might.
Waves of memory, gentle and warm,
Carving paths with every storm.

Every step a story unfolds,
In whispers soft, our journey holds.
Footprints linger, then fade away,
Yet in our hearts, they choose to stay.

Through fields of joy and valleys of pain,
Each imprint shows there's much to gain.
In laughter shared and tears we weep,
Footprints echo, our hearts keep.

Though paths diverge and miles may grow,
The essence of love we surely know.
With every footprint left behind,
Memories flourish, lovingly entwined.

As seasons change and years go by,
In our hearts, those footprints lie.
A testament to love's sweet part,
Forever etched, a work of art.

Milton Keynes UK
Ingram Content Group UK Ltd.
UKHW021929011224
451790UK00005B/87